SO-BAU-205

the I LOVE LUCY Guide to Life

the I LOVE LUCY

Guide to Life

WISDOM FROM LUCY AND THE GANG!

by Elisabeth Edwards

with Lucie Arnaz

RUNNING PRESS

PHILADELPHIA · LONDON

A Running Press Miniature Edition™

© 1998 by CBS Worldwide Inc. and Desilu, too, LLC

Printed in China

Library of Congress Cataloging-in-Publication Number 97-76141

ISBN 0-7624-0329-2

This book may be ordered by mail from the publisher. Please include $1.00 for postage and handling. *But try your bookstore first!*

Running Press Book Publishers
125 South Twenty-second Street
Philadelphia, Pennsylvania 19103-4399

Introduction

❤

On October 15, 1951, Lucille Ball, Desi Arnaz, Vivian Vance, and William Frawley made television history as they stepped on stage before a live audience for the premiere episode of the *I Love Lucy* show. Since that date, this classic show has never been off the air and is still seen today,

47 years later, in dozens of countries around the world. It is, in fact, the most re-run television show in history.

The secret behind the longevity of the show is its humanity. The Ricardos and the Mertzes taught the world about love, friendship, and loyalty. Whether at Kramer's Kandy Kitchen wrapping chocolates, in Los Angeles rubbing elbows with the stars, or in Italy stomping grapes, this fabulous foursome always managed to survive the wild antics that surrounded Lucy.

Desilu, too, LLC, and CBS Inc. are pleased to offer this book for the millions of fans, young and old, who have enjoyed this show for decades. Through the photos in this wonderful Miniature Edition™, Lucy, Ricky, Ethel, and Fred spring to life to reveal their secrets of staying together through good times and bad.

L   *R*   *E*   *F*

Try to fit in with the crowd.

Imitation

is the sincerest form of

flattery.

Lucy's Fashion Tips

#1

DON'T LET THIS HAPPEN TO YOU!

GOOD **HYGIENE** AND A SENSE OF **STYLE** ARE **ESSENTIAL!**

Always

try to get 8 hours of
beauty sleep ...

. . . or **face** the consequences!

Get up on the

right side

of the bed.

Tell the
truth
(when it
suits you!

Lucy Ricardo:
the Queen of SELECTIVE honesty!

When caught, deny
everything!

If it tastes **bad, it** must be **good** for you!

When in doubt,

ask!

A trim tummy keeps hubby happy!

Never send a

woman to do

a man's job...

. . . she just might do it

better!

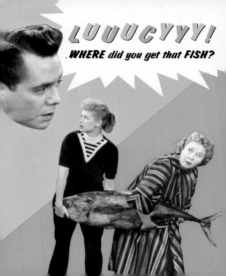

#2

Accessorize!

...without their wives.

ETHEL:
"I've heard 'em
say dozens of times
how hard it is to
get up a four-
some."

FRED:
"Oh brother!"

RICKY:
"Ai yi yi!"

LUCY:
"Gee, that's right. We'd really be doing them a favor."

If at first you don't succeed, try, try again.

Ricky, can I please be in your show? Please?
Please? Please? Pretty Please? Pretty please
with sugar on top? I swear I will never ask to
be in your show again. Oh please!!! You always
let the Mertz's in your show. Pleeeeeeeeeeease!
RICKY! ARE YOU LISTENING TO ME? Waaaaaa!
Waaaaaaaaaaa aaaaaaaaaaaaaa!
Please please e please. RICKY!
Please! Pleas e! Please! Just
this one time, I so much talent
and you just wo Please?Pretty
please with suga ease? Please?
Pleeeeeeee eeeeeeeeeeease!
Waaaaa aaaaa!
Please? lease?
Pleeee ease!
Waaa aaaa!

Where there's a will, there's a way!

Nobody likes a copycat.

MONKEY SEE,
MONKEY
DO!

If Lucy jumped off a bridge would you?

If your name happens to be

Ethel Mertz,
the answer is probably **YES!**

If you want something **done wrong,** do it yourself!

Home repair jobs are
for the birds!

Lucy's Fashion Tips

#3

Dress for Success!

Never be a
phone gossip!

Ethel, just WAIT 'til you hear the SCOOP on CAROLINE APPLEBY!

Crank calls are **never** amusing.

Misery loves company.

Laugh, and the
world laughs
with you...

. . . Weep, and you

weep alone.

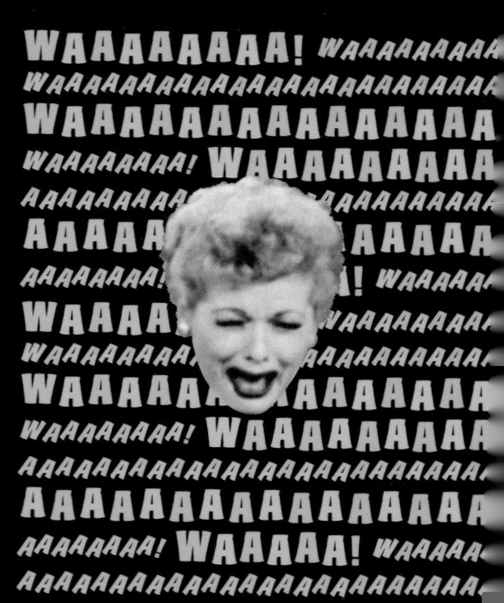

But, sometimes,
a good cry **does**
make it all better.

A smile is just
a frown turned
upside-down!

Mean
what
you
say!

Ricky Ricardo

When he says "No," he means "NO!!!"

Lucy's Fashion Tips

#4

DON'T BE A FASHION VICTIM!

Crime
doesn't pay.

SEE
NO EVIL

HEAR
NO EVIL

Lucy's Fashion Tips

#5

A nice tan
will add that
healthy
glow!

Get in touch with your
inner child.

You're **only** as old
as you **look**.

A penny saved is a penny earned

Fred Mertz:
self-proclaimed cheapskate!

Always leave

instructions

when putting someone
else in charge.

Beauty
is in the eye of the
beholder!

Clothes

MAKE

the man!

#7

Well, clothes don't

ALWAYS

make the man.

Beware

of princes—they can be

charming!

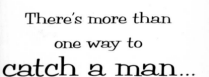

There's more than
one way to
catch a man...

. . . but only **one**
way to **keep** him!

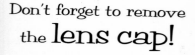

Don't forget to remove
the lens cap!

Patience is a virtue.

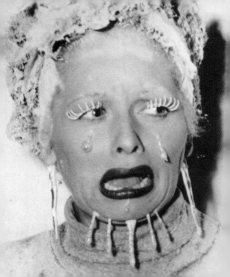

Always keep your cool.

Don't
antagonize
your spouse!

WATCH YOUR TEMPER!

Channel

your anger.

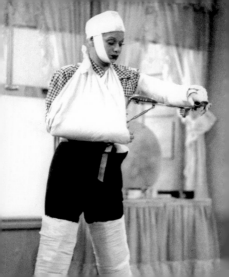

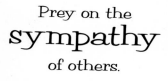

Prey on the **sympathy** of others.

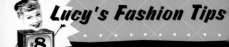

Lucy's Fashion Tips

#8

Ladies,

wax that

facial hair

before it's too late!